The World's Greatest Composers

Franz Schubert

by Barrie Carson Turner

OTHER TITLES IN THE SERIES
Johann Sebastian Bach by Charlotte Gray (1-85015-311-6)
Ludwig van Beethoven by Pam Brown (1-85015-302-7)
Leonard Bernstein by David Wilkins (1-85015-487-2)
Frederic Chopin by Pam Brown (1-85015-310-8)
Claude Debussy by Roderic Dunnett (1-85015-485-6)
Antonin Dvorak by Roderic Dunnett (1-85015-486-4)
Edvard Grieg by Wendy Thompson (1-85015-488-0)
Elton John by John O'Mahony (1-85015-369-8)
John Lennon by Michael White (1-85015-304-3)
Bob Marley by Marsha Bronson (1-85015-312-4)
Wolfgang Amadeus Mozart by Michael White (1-85015-300-0)
Peter Ilyich Tchaikovsky by Michael Pollard (1-85015-303-5)
Antonio Vivaldi by Pam Brown (1-85015-301-9)

Picture Credits
AKG/Berlin: cover; AKG/London: 5, 16, 19, 22, 23, 25, 30, 31, 36, 44, 48, 52(top); Art Resource/Erich Lessing: 4, 8, 9, 10, 12, 21, 26, 28, 33, 37, 41, 42, 43, 45, 46, 47, 49(left), 55, 58, 60; Edimedia: 14-15, 34-35, 49(right); Range/Bettmann: 15, 56; Ann Ronan/Image Select: 11, 20, 24, 29(top), 32, 39, 51, 52(bottom) 53, 54, 57; Spectrum Colour Library: 6, 18, 29, 38; Zefa: 50.

Extracts from *Schubert* by Peter Gammond used by kind permission of Methuen London.

Extracts from *Schubert, His Life His Work His Time* by Joseph Wechsberg used by kind permission of Weidenfeld and Nicolson.

Published in Great Britain in 1995
by Exley Publications Ltd,
16 Chalk Hill, Watford,
Herts WD1 4BN, United Kingdom.

A copy of the CIP data is available from the British Library on request.

ISBN 1-85015-494-5

Series editor: Samantha Armstrong
Editor: Helen Lanz
Editorial assistant: Alison MacTier
Musical adviser: Jill Simms
Picture editors: Alex Goldberg and James Clift of Image Select
Typeset by Delta Print, Watford, Herts, U.K.
Printed at Oriental Press, – UAE.

Franz SCHUBERT

by Barrie Carson Turner

EXLEY

Opposite: One of the best-known portraits of Franz Schubert. His main contribution to the musical world was in chamber and piano music and as a songwriter. Many of his compositions were well suited to the fashion of Hausmusik *(below). These private concerts became very popular in middle-class homes, and were made possible by increasing availability of the piano and of music for home use.*

Songwriter

There is almost no major musical form that the Viennese composer Franz Peter Schubert did not excel in, at some time in his brief life, whether it was piano or chamber music, symphonies or vocal music.

But it is to the world of song that Schubert makes his greatest musical contribution as a composer and for which he is so widely known.

At the turn of the nineteenth century no great composer, with the possible exception of Beethoven, had written many songs. But for Schubert, from the start of his schoolboy composing years, songwriting was his first love. He created a musical medium that was taken up by later German songwriters, such as Schumann, Mendelssohn, and Brahms. He developed a new style of piano accompaniment – it now shared equal importance with the voice. All of Schubert's piano parts were highly imaginative, and while the accompaniment and song were usually interlinked, some of the parts were considered to be piano pieces in their own right.

Schubert was also gifted as a melodist. Each composition, whether for instruments or voices, is filled with memorable, singable tunes. So impressive is the wealth of melody running through his works that, to many critics and writers, he will always be the greatest melodist of all time.

Looking for success

One musical element, however, that brought Schubert little or no acclaim was the opera. The skills required to build a dramatic work for a two or

The Music Association in Vienna, which was formed in 1812 to promote music. In June 1827 Schubert was elected to its membership – an important step for a musician who wanted to find recognition among the Austrian public.

three hour performance always eluded him, although he wrote stage works almost to the end of his life.

In 1818, when Schubert returned from a teaching appointment in the household of Count Esterházy in Hungary, he learned that a singer friend, Michael Vogl, had managed to secure a commission for him to write a new opera.

This was to be a one-act farce called *Die Zwillingsbrüder – The Twin Brothers* – and Vogl was to take the male lead – singing the parts of both brothers. Schubert was delighted. Here was a chance to convince the Viennese musical society of his skills as an opera composer. If he could do this – success was his. He eagerly set to work and completed the score in about two months.

Uproar

It was not until a year later that the opera was performed. At the time Vienna was intoxicated with the music of the Italian opera composer Rossini, and while the near-frenzy lasted Rossini operas filled the city. However, the first evening performance of *Die Zwillingsbrüder,* on June 14, 1820, at the *Kärntnertor Theater,* finally came. It was Franz Schubert's first major work to be performed in public.

Yet the evening that seemed to have such promise ended strangely. Schubert's friends and colleagues were in the audience and they led the applause. And what applause! They cheered the music and performers whenever there was the slightest excuse. Unfortunately, the remainder of the audience was decidedly less than happy at this show of appreciation. A scuffle between Schubert's friends and some of the audience threatened to break out. "Schubert's friends made a lot of noise," one eye-witness reported, "while the opposition hissed."

At the close of the performance the audience was alive with tension until Michael Vogl came on stage and, apologizing for the composer's absence, thanked the audience for its attention. In fact, Schubert had watched the performance, but was high in the gallery arguing loudly with friends who wanted him to change his ordinary frock-coat for a more formal tailcoat so he would look more presentable for the curtain call. The composer saw no reason why he should change his clothes simply to make a public appearance – it was his music that was important, not what he was wearing.

"In his [Schubert's] short lifetime he produced masterworks in a number of genres and established himself as one of the greatest songwriters in Western musical history."

Philip D. Morehead, from Bloomsbury Dictionary of Music.

Respect

Later, in Lenkays wine shop, Schubert and his friends were toasting his success. But when the reviews of the concert appeared it was obvious that the work had only been received relatively well.

"Schubert has done himself credit with his first opera but is not yet approaching the summit of Parnassus," said one critic. Another particularly vicious critic commented on Schubert's unruly friends. Others hinted there wasn't a good tune in the whole piece and that Schubert had no sense of drama. However, the show ran for six performances.

"The House of the Red Crab"

In many families, in Schubert's time as well as today, sons are often named after their fathers. This was the case in the Schubert household. In 1796, Schubert's father, Franz Theodor Schubert, and his wife,

"Even as a boy, Schubert lived an introspective intellectual life which never expressed itself in words, but almost always only in music."
Franz Eckel, Flautist of the Konvikt *orchestra.*

Elizabeth, moved into a lodging house in the *Himmelpfortgrund* district of Vienna in Austria. The building had the curious name of *Zum Roten Krebsen – At the Red Crab.*

It was divided into sixteen apartments, each consisting of one room and a tiny kitchen. The Schuberts were luckier than most of the other lodgers as they had two apartments joined together. In the two larger rooms of the apartment, Franz Theodor accommodated the one hundred and eighty pupils who made up the school he ran there.

Money problems

Schubert's father was both the head teacher and administrator of the school. The classes were divided into two groups: half the pupils attended a morning session, and the other half an afternoon session. The school was not well equipped and conditions were cramped. But there were many other problems, for besides having to teach the poorer children for no payment at all, it was up to Franz Theodor to extract

Franz Theodor Schubert, the composer's father, was a devout Roman Catholic and a dedicated schoolteacher. Although he was never completely happy with his son's choice of career, it was through him that Schubert was first introduced to music.

whatever fees he could from the others. All the school bills had to be paid before he could draw his own small salary on which he had to support his family.

The Schuberts had eight children who did not survive beyond the age of six. In late eighteenth century Vienna the number of children who died was very high, especially in poor families. However, three boys – Ignaz, Ferdinand, and Franz Karl – and a daughter, Maria, survived infancy. It was into this busy household that, on the last day of January 1797, a fourth son, Franz Peter, was born.

"The House of the Red Crab" where Schubert was born. The building later became a Schubert Museum, with the property restored to its original appearance as Schubert would have known it. The Schuberts lived here for sixteen years and left when Franz was four.

Early talent

When Franz was four years old, the Schuberts moved the school to new premises with more space for the growing number of pupils. All the Schubert children attended the school. When they reached a suitable age they were encouraged to become assistant teachers to help keep costs down.

Franz was just six years old when his father

"I was very astonished when, after only a few months, he told me he no longer needed any further tuition from me, and that he now wanted to manage by himself. And within a short space of time he made such progress that I was obliged to recognize him as a master who had far surpassed me and whose standard I could no longer acclaim."

Ignaz Schubert.

recognized his son's musical abilities. He taught Franz the violin, while Ignaz, now a seventeen year old assistant teacher, gave his brother piano lessons. By the age of nine, Franz was well on the way to outstripping both his brother and his father.

He was also composing short pieces, and the family played them in the quartet they formed. Franz played the viola, his father the cello, and Ignaz and Ferdinand the violins. Although Franz was the youngest performer in the group, he was unquestionably in charge, pointing out his father's wrong notes or rhythms – pleasantly, but firmly. These early compositions were created at a remarkable speed considering the noisy family background that the young composer had to endure.

First teachers

When Franz had outgrown his family teachers, his father sent him to the choirmaster of the parish church at Liechtental for lessons. Here the ten year

Schubert took his keyboard lessons at the organ of the parish church at Liechtental. On the music stand is a manuscript by Haydn, whose music greatly influenced Schubert's early compositions.

old continued his lessons on the violin and piano, and his new teacher, Michael Holzer, *tried* to teach him the organ, singing, and harmony. "If I wanted to instruct him in anything new, he already knew it," Holzer recalled. "Therefore I gave him no actual tuition but merely talked to him and watched him with silent astonishment."

The year 1808 was of great importance for Franz Peter Schubert. His father had been looking for a new educational opportunity for his son, since the boy had clearly outgrown the skills of Michael Holzer. A soprano voice was required immediately for the Imperial Court Chapel. The successful applicant would also receive instruction in general subjects, as well as music, at the *Kaiserlich-königliches Stadtkonvikt* – the Imperial and Royal City College. This was the most respected school in Vienna and a chance the young Franz could not miss.

Schubert, with his fine singing voice, was one of ten singers in the Imperial Court Chapel. There were places for eighteen choirboys at the school.

Actions, not appearances

Accordingly, father and son attended the auditions. Each applicant was expected to demonstrate a solid grounding in Latin, display a superior singing voice, and have a knowledge of composition. The examining panel included the court *Kapellmeister,* Antonio Salieri, who for forty years had held the prestigious position of being the most important musician in Vienna.

Schubert was determined to present his son as elegantly as money would allow and dressed him in a pale blue – almost white – frock-coat. This caused some mirth among the other boys, who mocked the over-indulgent dress sense, dubbing Franz "the miller's son." But to the examiners, the clothes Franz was wearing were not important. The auditioning panel only heard his exquisitely clear soprano voice. There was no question of not admitting a pupil of such talent to the choir.

So, within a few weeks, dressed in a uniform of brown coat, white breeches, smart shoes, and a distinguished three-cornered hat with gold braid, Franz Peter Schubert took his place among some of the finest young singing voices in Vienna.

School-days

Life as a boarder at the *Konvikt,* as the school was known, was not easy – and eleven year old Franz found parting with his family hard. The pupils were rarely allowed home, and he only saw his parents when he was performing his official choir duties. General lessons occupied his daytime studies – Latin, mathematics, history, natural history, physics, geography, and religious instruction. Music lessons were held in the evenings.

The school food was always poor and seldom sufficient, so a constant hunger – and cold, for the classrooms were never warm – formed the backdrop to the young composer's music making. There was very little spare time, since duties as a chorister also had to be fitted in. What little free time he had, Franz Schubert gave over to composing. He was determined that, above all else, he must always find time for this.

His first term at the *Konvikt* ended on April 17, 1809. The reports from his teachers were good. The director of the school – Innocenz Lang, a stern disciplinarian who often terrified his pupils – said

At the Stadtkonvikt, *where Schubert studied from the age of eleven to sixteen, the boys had lessons in music theory, as well as in general subjects. Schubert was often praised for his studies and was especially good at singing, and playing the piano and the violin.*

that Franz had "a musical talent." This was to appear on most of Franz's reports for the full five years that he spent at the school.

Lifelong friend

Almost as soon as he started at the *Konvikt,* Franz started playing second violin in the school orchestra, and later went on to lead the first violins. The orchestra consisted of strings, as well as flutes, oboes, clarinets, bassoons, horns, trumpets, and drums. It was at one rehearsal that Franz met and became friends with a law student at the university, Josef von Spaun, who was nine years his senior. Spaun had originally formed the *Konvikt* orchestra and still played in it.

After one rehearsal, Spaun found the composer working alone in one of the music rooms. Schubert put aside the Mozart sonata he was studying and played a minuet he had composed himself. Spaun was astounded by the compositional skill of the eleven year old. Later, when Franz could not afford to buy the quantities of manuscript paper he needed, the elder student supplied it. This was the first of many kindnesses shown by Spaun to Schubert. It was also the beginning of a friendship that was to last all of the composer's short life.

Orchestral experience

Through playing in the orchestra, Franz Schubert became acquainted with the symphonies of Haydn, Beethoven, and Mozart. He particularly liked Mozart's great G minor Symphony. But in the Viennese musical circles of the time other composers were also fashionable, such as Kenner, who is almost unheard of today.

During rehearsals of Kenner's and similar music, Schubert would repeatedly say, "Oh, how boring!" and question why the orchestra performed this kind of music, while the symphonies of Haydn were just waiting to be played.

Occasionally the school orchestra attempted much harder music, sometimes by Beethoven, of which

"With the classical works of the greatest masters Schubert was intimately acquainted, and he felt for them – for Handel, Gluck, Mozart, Haydn and Beethoven – the most enthusiastic reverence."

A friend, after Schubert's death.

Schubert greatly approved. He found that by playing in an orchestra, he could hear – and learn – how the composer wrote for each individual instrument.

As well as playing in the orchestra, Schubert was given the position of "orchestral assistant." By all accounts this was a rather uninspiring position. It involved looking after the instruments, maintaining the stocks of music in good, clean condition, setting up the room for each rehearsal session, and lighting the candles. However, it was worth every bit of dreary work because the music teacher, Herr Ruzicka, occasionally allowed Schubert to conduct the orchestra in his absence.

This meant that, at the age of thirteen, Franz Schubert had to master the orchestral techniques needed to conduct pieces by Beethoven and Mozart. It also meant that he could get the orchestra to play his own compositions.

Early works

Most of Schubert's early compositions consisted of chamber music, or works written for a small group of instruments. He had already acquired a good knowledge of chamber music by studying scores with his composition teacher and playing in small instrumental combinations with friends.

For Schubert the important thing was that chamber music had a better chance of being played. It was no great problem to assemble a group of friends to play through any new compositions. Few of these early compositions have survived. However, the music for his *Fantasia* for Piano Duet, written during March and April in 1810, when he was only thirteen, has survived. The Six Minuets for wind instruments, written the following year, also remain.

It is not surprising that these schoolboy works show the influence of established composers – especially Haydn and Mozart, whose symphonies featured so often in the *Konvikt* orchestra's repertoire. But the influence of Beethoven – not even at the peak of his career yet – is also there. Schubert experimented, as Beethoven did, with unusual modulations – or changes of key – and harmonic sequences.

Background: The autographed manuscript of the song Jägars Abendlied – Gamekeeper's Love Song, *written in 1816 during one of the periods when Schubert was trying to leave teaching. The words of the song are by the German poet Goethe, whose poetry Schubert came increasingly to admire and on which he based much of his music.*

Joseph Haydn, one of the composers whose music Schubert enjoyed playing in the Konvikt *orchestra. On summer evenings, passers-by often gathered outside the* Konvikt *music room to listen to the rehearsals.*

A quiet boy?

Although composition was a solitary occupation, requiring quiet and, to some extent, withdrawal from other social activities, Schubert also enjoyed the company of his school friends.

His school friend Georg Franz Eckel remembered Schubert as "shy and uncommunicative." On school outings he could often be seen by himself, completely absorbed in his own private thoughts. Physically, Schubert was short and stocky with broad shoulders, brown curly hair, and brown eyes. He wore glasses most of the time, and had a habit of squinting. He had a friendly, round face with a predominent forehead and chin. Another friend recalled that he "never laughed openly and fully, but only managed a chuckle which sounded toneless rather than bright."

The Emperor Napoleon led the French army twice against Austria during the Napoleonic Wars of 1805–1815. Vienna came under siege on both occasions. In 1809, when Schubert was twelve, the city was heavily attacked by canon fire as the Austrians tried to reassert their control, only to lose to Napoleon later that year at the Battle of Wagram.

Family conflict

Schubert knew that his father was against him becoming a composer full time. His father was determined that he should have the best available education, and was happy to have his son's musical gifts nurtured, but this was only to be in preparation for taking up a post in an "acceptable" profession. Being a composer was not acceptable – being a schoolteacher was.

In short, his father intended that Schubert should eventually work for him as an assistant teacher. Over the past years, while Schubert had been studying at the *Konvikt,* the school had grown considerably. From one hundred and eighty pupils and only one assistant, the number was up to almost three hundred pupils and six assistants. Teaching was a "real profession" – and one with social standing.

Napoleon

Futhermore, this was no time to become a composer. Schubert had been born into troubled times in Austria. The Napoleonic Wars were raging across Europe. In 1805, the capital of Austria, Vienna, had been occupied by Napoleon's French army. The Austrian

troops had a small victory against the invaders, but by 1809 there had been a second invasion. These times of political uncertainty brought about many changes to the way of life and culture of the city, and the effects were widespread. The wealthy Viennese patrons of music, with their financial support of musicians like Schubert, were fast disappearing.

Schubert, however, was not convinced by these arguments and in 1810 he and his father had a serious quarrel. Schubert's friend Spaun spoke of a "storm" between the two parties, during which time Schubert became withdrawn and unusually serious. There were hints that Schubert was even forbidden from entering the family house.

"Hagars Klage"

As a boy, and throughout his life, Franz Schubert was an avid reader. At the *Konvikt* he was intellectually advanced for his years, and most of the literature and poetry he read was far beyond the capabilities of his school friends.

He constantly made notes of verses that attracted him. He was particularly excited by the poems of the German writer Friedrich von Schiller. It was said that Schiller's poetry was impossible to set to music, yet Schubert was to compose a number of songs based on Schiller's poems.

Schubert also experimented with writing for the voice from an early age. On March 30, 1811, when he was fourteen, he composed a work that was to be the first in the long line of songs for which he would be most remembered as a composer. It was a song called *Hagars Klage – Hagar's Lament* – with words by another German poet, Levin Schücking. When Schubert's teacher Wenzel Ruzicka showed the song to the court *Kapellmeister*, Antonio Salieri, he was so impressed that he invited Schubert to study with him.

It was also during this year that Schubert went to his first opera. On July 8, Spaun took Schubert to see Joseph Weigl's *Die Schweizerfamilie* at the *Kärntnertor-Theater*. This visit marked the beginning of an operatic passion in Schubert that would last his lifetime and influence his style of composition.

"He [Schubert] was the first composer to make harmony and the accompaniment as important as the melody and the words of the poem. It has been said that in Schubert's hands all poetry became music."

Joseph Wechsberg, from Schubert – His Life His Work His Time.

Death in the family

Only the following year, in 1812, Schubert's mother, Elizabeth, became unwell, and on May 28, she died. With the entire running of the business of the school now falling on his father's shoulders alone, Schubert was in even more demand to help by becoming an assistant teacher. Spaun – a constant emotional prop to Schubert – collected a number of reports praising Schubert's compositions to show his father in the hope of convincing him that his talented son would be wasted as a teacher.

In the summer of that year came another major change in Schubert's life – his voice began to break. On his copy of the mass that the choir was performing at the time, fifteen year old Schubert scrawled, "Schubert, Franz, crowed for the last time, July 26, 1812."

The outcome of this was clear – Franz Schubert would have to leave the choir. He might have been asked to leave the school entirely were it not for his academic skills which convinced the authorities that he could stay on and continue his studies.

Although not devout by nature, Schubert admitted to having strong religious feelings that sometimes overcame him. The many beautiful buildings of Vienna, such as the inside of Maria am Gestade *Church (right), were a source of religious inspiration to him.*

Antonio Salieri, who had at one time been Beethoven's teacher, was himself a composer of some standing. Although Schubert was initially very pleased to be invited to take lessons with the great master, their teacher-pupil relationship soon became strained over differences in musical taste.

Learning his craft

Although Schubert attended the *Konvikt* primarily as a chorister, he also studied other areas of music while he was there. Of major interest to him were subjects that were most related to composition.

It seems his lessons with the great Salieri may have been something of a disappointment. In preparation for his first lesson, Schubert had taken a sheet of manuscript paper and written on the top of it, "Began counterpoint [the study of how to write music in parts] on June 18, 1812." A few sessions later, the lessons had only consisted of reading and playing through scores, and completing small harmony exercises.

Moreover, Salieri, being Italian, was interested in Italian styles of composition. Schubert, however, was passionately involved with German and Austrian music and literature.

More than once, teacher and pupil argued. A major stumbling block between them was their differences of taste in literature and the unflattering remarks that Salieri constantly made about the poets Schubert loved most. He insisted their "barbarous words" were not fit to be set to music. He gave Schubert Italian texts to set to music, even though his pupil could barely understand the language.

Escape from prison

Although Schubert continued to make remarkable strides as a budding musician while studying at the *Konvikt,* he was not entirely happy there. When Spaun left to study law Schubert shouted after him, "You're escaping from prison, you lucky fellow."

In November 1812, a year before leaving himself, Schubert wrote a teasing letter to his brother Ferdinand, inventing a few references to the Bible to support his cause: "Life is pretty good, but in some ways it could be better.... You know, a roll or a few apples would not come amiss in the eight and a half hours between a middling lunch and a miserable dinner.... The few groschen I receive from father vanishes in the first few days, so what am I going to do for the rest of the time? 'They who hope upon Him shall not be put to shame,' Matthew 3:4. How true!

"How would it be then if you were to let me have a few kreutzer each month? You wouldn't notice this

More than any other member of the the family, Schubert's elder brother Ferdinand was responsible for offering constant help and friendship to Schubert, most particularly during the prolonged period of the composer's illness and before his early death.

amount, and the money would make me happy and contented in my cell. I repeat and reaffirm the words of the Apostle Matthew when he says, 'Let he who hath two coats give one to the poor,' etc. So I hope that you will heed the voice that ever calls upon you to remember your loving, poor, hopeful, and yet again poor – and not to be forgotten brother, Franz."

Freedom at last

The next year, despite his unhappiness at the school, Schubert found time to devote himself to music, and used his private study periods for composing. He planned to stay at the *Konvikt* for another year, but was not happy with the low priority given to music. He struggled on for another few months until, at the age of sixteen, he finally decided to leave the school.

As a tribute to the *Konvikt,* Franz dedicated his First Symphony, completed on October 28, 1813, to the director, Dr. Lang. The symphony was performed by the same *Konvikt* orchestra in which Schubert had played.

A portrait of Schubert in his mid-twenties. The composer's physical appearance in paintings tended to vary enormously, and he was portrayed in a more flattering light after his death. This painting is unusual in that it shows him without his glasses, which were essential to him in his daily life.

Teacher training

The family celebrated when Schubert returned home. His father had remarried that year and Schubert's stepmother, Anna Kleyenböck, was only fourteen years older than he was. His stepmother was very good to him, occasionally helping him out financially with money saved from her own housekeeping. His father was thrilled because Schubert seemed to be following his advice at last.

Schubert was then immediately entered for a teacher training course at St. Anna's College for the academic year 1813–1814. In the October that he left school, Schubert had written a piece and dedicated it to his father. It was a cantata, a vocal piece for choir or several voices, for which he had also written the words. Now that Schubert had agreed to join the family establishment, his father was willing to accept the importance of composition in his son's life.

Above: Financial problems caused the composer to return to the classroom, teaching at his father's school, similar in style to this one, on several occasions during his lifetime.

Assistant teacher

But Schubert's heart was not in his teacher training studies, and it was only with some difficulty that he passed the final examination. During the year, he tried for military conscription, but was turned down because he was less than five feet tall (1.5m). In the end, he achieved the pass mark at the college, and much to his father's satisfaction, on August 19, 1814, the seventeen year old joined the school as its newest assistant teacher.

As a composer, Schubert had infinite patience, but as a teacher he had very little, and with six year old children he had even less! He taught the lowest age group in the school, and on occasion resorted to using the cane. The worst deed his charges could commit was to disturb him while he was composing.

Composing habits

If Schubert composed during lesson times it is most likely to have been without his father's knowledge. Certainly he had the rare ability to compose regardless of noise and movement around him. He found that he could write surprisingly quickly. "Completed in 4½ hours" is scribbled on the manuscript of the first movement of his String Quartet in B flat. One friend recalled, "If you go to see him during the day, he says, 'Hello, how are you? – Good!' and goes on working, whereupon you go away." Schubert seldom used the piano when composing. He would sit at his writing desk, bite his pen, and drum his fingers. His poor sight caused him to bend closely over his manuscript.

Schubert continued to take lessons with his old teacher, Salieri, for another two years after leaving the *Konvikt*. He met his *Konvikt* friends regularly throughout this period, often at musical evenings of their own devising, at which Schubert's works were

Opposite: The original manuscript of Schubert's song Die Taubenpost – The Pigeon Post. *Many of Schubert's compositions were written in the time it took to put pen to paper, and he never revised anything that he didn't like. His friends said that he could be inspired at any time, even while sharing a coffee together.*

played. His old friend Josef von Spaun treated Schubert to concerts and visits to the opera. Most times they sat in the cheapest seats, enjoying supper together after the performance.

Public acclaim

In May 1814, Schubert had begun working on a new piece – his Mass in F – to be performed at the centenary celebrations of the Liechtental church. This work was completed on July 22, and as soon as the parts had been copied out, rehearsals began. The first performance was on October 16, and it was a very grand affair.

Schubert conducted, while the church choir sang to the organ, played by his brother Ferdinand. The performance immediately brought Schubert

Therese Grob, who as a young girl sang at the first performance of Schubert's Mass in F. Her fine singing voice, together with Michael Holzer's well-trained choir, contributed greatly to the success of the two performances of the work.

considerable public acclaim. The Mass was given a second performance ten days later. The soprano solo was sung by Therese Grob, a local girl still in her mid-teens. She had a beautiful soprano voice. The Schubert and Grob families had known each other for some years and Schubert found himself falling in love with Therese, but the affair did not develop. Therese later married a wealthy local baker.

This exciting time in Schubert's life coincided with the end of the Napoleonic Wars, which had been raging in Europe, and the Congress of Vienna, which outlined the peace settlement made between the major European powers.

In Austria, however, the freedom of the people was to be increasingly curbed under the iron rule of Emperor Franz I and his chancellor, Prince Metternich. From this time, Austria suffered strong censorship of books, newspapers, and the arts.

First songs

By the end of 1814 Schubert already had a considerable number of compositions to his name and he was still only seventeen. Besides his First Symphony and the Mass in F, he had written over fifty songs and six string quartets. He had also written church music, an octet for wind instruments, minuets and dances for various combinations of instruments, piano sonatas and fantasias, overtures, and an opera in three acts.

He had written more songs than any other compositions and was increasingly interested in literature, especially poetry, sometimes also writing the words to accompany his music. When he was attracted to or impressed by a poem, he immediately wanted to express it musically.

In the first twenty years of the nineteenth century, music moved away from the courts and salons and became more available to the general public. There was a big craze for waltzes, and Schubert wrote a lot of dance music at this time. He could have made friends with the wealthy and famous people in Vienna, but he preferred to make friends with artists. Many of his friends were poets and writers, and it

was quite common for them to offer their work for him to set to music. The poet Johann Mayrhofer said his poems only seemed to come to life when they had been set to music by Schubert.

After the defeat of Napoleon in 1815, the countries of Austria, Great Britain, Russia, and France met at the Congress of Vienna to redraw the European map, giving back territories that had been lost in the wars. The peace that the Congress created in Europe lasted for the next forty years.

The songs Schubert was writing were in a completely new style. Great importance was placed on the words, and especially on how their meaning was linked to the piano accompaniment and the melody. Schubert composed so that the piano accompaniment described what was happening dramatically in the poetry. Today Schubert's songs and those written in the same style are referred to as "lieder." This German word simply means "songs."

"Gretchen at the Spinning Wheel"

October 19, 1814, was a very important day for Franz Schubert. Within the space of a few hours the composer had written what was to be one of his most memorable and acclaimed songs, *Gretchen am Spinnrade – Gretchen at the Spinning Wheel.*

Schubert took the words from the poem *Faust,* by the German writer and poet Goethe. In this song a young woman sits spinning as she thinks and daydreams of the man she loves. Over the flowing piano accompaniment – which represents the spinning wheel – she sings a sad, but beautiful melody. When she stops suddenly, at the high point of the poem, the piano stops too. Then the momentum of the song is regained gradually as the spinning wheel resumes its whirring motion.

New friends

Franz Schubert's circle of friends and admirers was now widening – with thanks particularly to Josef von Spaun, who introduced the young composer to an ever-increasing number of artists and writers.

His closest friends often met at the family home – to the great disapproval of Schubert's father, who saw Spaun and the others as having a bad influence on his son. He was determined that music would not draw his son away from teaching again.

Occasionally Schubert and his friends would meet at the *Konvikt* – to the displeasure of the directors who disapproved of any rowdiness, no matter how

A group of close friends and intellectuals followed Schubert's music and would hear him play his new compositions in their own homes.

good-natured, disturbing the peace of the school corridors. The appointed day for visiting the *Konvikt* was usually Sunday. Sometimes while the others were in church, Schubert would be locked in one of the music rooms with a pen, paper, and a volume of poems. When the church service was over, his colleagues would rush in to inspect what Schubert had written during their absence.

Schubert was often a little too relaxed about lending or giving away his manuscripts. Spaun told a story about Schubert's carelessness: "In 1812 Franz composed twelve extraordinarily beautiful minuets and trios. He passed the manuscripts from one person to another until finally they vanished!

"No one knew who had them last. He [Franz] was very annoyed, and intended to write the pieces out again, but he put the job off too long, until in the end the music slipped from his memory...." In later years, another friend, Albert Stadler, took it upon himself to make copies of many of Schubert's songs – and it is probably due to him that so many beautiful works have survived to the present day.

A remarkable year

It is almost impossible to believe that during 1815, while Schubert was fully involved with teaching, he still found time to write two hundred new works.

He began the year by completing his Second Symphony, begun the previous December, and on May 24 he started work on his Third Symphony, finishing it on July 19 of the same year. He also wrote 145 new songs, writing six in one day, including the famous *Heidenröslein*. It was an astoundingly productive year.

Toward the close of 1815 Schubert wrote what is probably his best-known song, *Erlkönig – The Erl King*. When the song was complete, he and Spaun immediately set off for the *Konvikt* to play it on one of the school pianos. Schubert never seemed to have enough money to buy his own piano and could never even afford to rent one.

Many of Schubert's songs were first performed at small, informal social gatherings. The evenings

"If Schubert ... was not the greatest of all composers, he was, surely, the great magician of them all in turning those black dots on five undeviating lines into a moving expression of the human spirit."

Peter Gammon, from Schubert.

Congregating in inns and alehouses was a popular pastime in Vienna in the early nineteenth century. Schubert was a great socializer, and almost every evening he met his close circle of friends at the inns and coffeehouses in and around the Austrian capital. Such places were sometimes locations for music-making as well. The drinking sessions often went on late into the night.

usually began with a poetry reading before the musical entertainment began. Colleagues and friends would usually finish off the evening with a drinking session at a local inn – often not returning home until the early hours.

It was during this year that Schubert met a wealthy law student named Franz von Schober. Schober was impressed with Schubert's gifts as a composer, and spent a considerable time trying to persuade his new friend to leave teaching. Whereas Schober's finances were assured, however, Schubert's were not. Much as Schubert passionately wanted to follow his chosen career, he had to find a means of support.

"Erlkönig"

One performance of *Erlkönig,* with Schubert playing the piano himself, was particularly interesting. The accompaniment for this song is notoriously difficult and Schubert was noticed to be "cheating" by

substituting the difficult repeated triplets with an easier version. Some *Konvikt* teachers present asked him why he had omitted the triplets. "They are too difficult for me," he replied, "but a virtuoso would be able to play them!"

The song is based on another of Goethe's poems and is a masterpiece of drama and excitement. Goethe took the legend of the *Erlkönig* from Danish folklore. The story tells of the Erl King living deep in the Black Forest who, with soft-spoken entreaties and promises, lures the spirits of children to their doom. In the poem, a father speeds through the night on horseback carrying a young child. Over and over again the child cries out in fear, hearing the Erl King's whisperings and temptations. The father reassures the child – it is only the wind and the rain. But when the rider reaches his destination, the child is dead in his arms.

Above: The first page of Erlkönig – The Erl King, *showing a simplified arrangement of Schubert's piano accompaniment without the difficult triplets of the first version.*

Below: Goethe, one of the greatest German playwrights and poets of Schubert's time.

Seeking approval

In April 1816 Spaun sent sixteen of Schubert's songs to Goethe, including *Erlkönig* and *Gretchen am Spinnrade,* in the hope that the poet would approve them. Each song had been copied carefully by Schubert in his neatest hand, and the collection had been impressively bound together. Spaun's accompanying letter introduced the nineteen year old Schubert, and begged that the poet would consent to the collection being dedicated to him. Spaun indicated the already growing popularity of the songs, and, somewhat stretching the truth, hinted at further volumes of songs dedicated to other poets of standing. The volume was returned without comment. However, some fifteen years later, in response to *Erlkönig,* Goethe added, "I have heard this composition once before, when it did not appeal to me at all; but sung in this way the whole shapes itself into a visible picture."

The symphonies of Beethoven were considered great works and were popular with Viennese society in the nineteenth century. Although Schubert took inspiration from Haydn and Mozart in his early works, he later drew more from the compositions of this great master.

Trying to move on

By the spring of 1816, Schubert had been a teacher for eighteen months. He hated the hard work, which paid very little. So he applied for a music post at a training school for teachers, with a better salary. He submitted an impressive testimonial from Salieri, but failed to get the position.

Yet 1816, like 1815, was another very productive year. His output included over one hundred new songs – among them the well known *Wiegenlied – Cradlesong*. He wrote and dedicated a new mass to his old teacher, Michael Holzer.

In April he completed his Fourth Symphony, which he named the *Tragic,* after its gloomy opening theme. In this symphony, Schubert starts to break new ground. Since writing the first three symphonies he had become more familiar with Beethoven's compositions, and it was his strongest wish to use the skills he felt he had learned from Vienna's most distinguished living composer in his own music.

Beethoven

To Schubert, Beethoven was the greatest of all composers. Throughout his life he went to concerts of Beethoven's music whenever he could afford to.

Once he sold some books in order to buy a ticket to see Beethoven's opera, *Fidelio*.

Schubert longed to meet the composer, but this was only to occur once – on Beethoven's deathbed. There were occasions when he met Beethoven in the street, but he was always overcome by a terrible shyness and found he couldn't make an approach.

Schubert used the musical style of the older composer in many elements of his work. In the Fourth Symphony, for example, the four-note rhythm that is so important throughout the work is reminiscent of the dominating rhythmic figure of Beethoven's Fifth Symphony. It is also interesting to note that both these symphonies were the composers' first ones to be written in the minor key – and the *same* minor key.

Writing for money

Schubert did not keep a diary. However, for brief periods in his life he wrote down his thoughts and feelings. On June 17, 1816, he wrote, "Today I composed for money for the first time. Namely a cantata, words by Dräxler, for Prof. Watteroth's name day. The fee is 100 Viennese florins."

Professor Watteroth, a friend of Spaun's, was a teacher of law at the university. His students had planned a festive occasion for him. The theme was to be the Greek god Prometheus, who stole fire from heaven to improve the lot of humankind. Schubert was very excited about the commission, once more obtained through Spaun. The fee offered was over twice the amount of his annual teacher's salary!

The performance of *Prometheus* brought Schubert a very important new contact – Leopold von Sonnleithner. The Sonnleithners held considerable influence in Viennese musical society. Leopold ran an orchestra that had no private patron and so had greater freedom in the music it chose to play. It was purely amateur and was supported by subscriptions from its participants. Its membership did include some professional musicians, but it consisted mainly of tradespeople with modest incomes.

The orchestra had become quite popular, making

The Greek god Prometheus was punished by the ruler of the gods, Zeus, for stealing fire for the human race. Prometheus suffered the gruesome fate of being chained to a high rocky peak, where an eagle pecked at his liver by day, which would then regrow by night.

"For giving lessons, as Mozart had done, Schubert had neither the gift nor patience. His bitter experience in youth as a schoolmaster put him off trying this method of bringing grist to the mill. Rather starve and be free to dream, to sing and compose as an independent artist!"

An account of Schubert.

its own small income from the sale of tickets. But the money received from this was not enough to pay for composers to create pieces especially for it. All Schubert could hope to make from performances of his music by the orchestra, besides the pleasure of hearing his own works performed and enjoyed by others, was the occasional useful musical contact and what public acclaim the performances of his works brought him.

Peace at last

Schubert's friends were also eager to help the young composer where they could, and none more so than Franz von Schober. Schober persuaded Schubert to take up an offer of rooms in his mother's house. Here Schober's mother and sister made the nineteen year old very welcome. His living conditions improved remarkably. There was space and peace – he no longer had to put up with a crowded family home with its continuous noise and disruptive children.

At last he could follow his passion for composing without being disturbed by his father's constant disapproving comments. "I should have become nothing but a thwarted musician," Schubert said of staying at home and teaching. So the ties with teaching and the old family home were cut.

This new connection also proved very useful. It was through Schober that Schubert came into contact with the highly respected singer, Michael Vogl.

Johann Michael Vogl was a well-known singer at the Vienna Opera before he met Schubert. Vogl and Schubert became firm friends – each admiring the other's talent.

An important meeting

Schubert had heard Vogl sing at the Vienna opera four years earlier. Now Schober had arranged a meeting with the great man in person especially for Schubert, who was very nervous about it.

The day came and Vogl arrived promptly at Schober's apartment. Schubert felt terribly embarrassed, making an awkward little bow and expressing his pleasure at meeting the great man. Vogl, large and portly, simply towered over

A portrait of one of Schubert's closest friends, the poet and actor Franz von Schober, whom Schubert met in 1814. In friendship, they often referred to themselves as "Schobert." Through Schober, Schubert met many influential writers and artists.

Schubert. However, the singer agreed to try one of Franz Schubert's songs with the composer accompanying him. He hummed the song – he was barely singing – and commented, "Not bad." Then he asked to see more of Schubert's work. When the meeting was over, he left saying that Schubert did not make the most of his gifts.

But the fifty year old singer clearly liked the young composer – and his music.

Who you know

Vogl and Schubert met again, and within a short time became friends. Vogl's days in the opera were coming to an end and the prospect of performing at occasional evening parties with Schubert seemed rather attractive – a pleasant alternative to the pressures of the opera house.

In later years Vogl did much to promote Schubert's work, although on occasions he took liberties with the music – by transposing the key up or down, adding flourishes, or at times even changing some of the actual notes! To Schubert this

Following page: Schubert's informal gatherings of friends or "Schubertiads" became a focal point for his music. His compositions of chamber music, sonatas, songs, piano solos, and duets were ideal for such events. In this way his works gradually became known in Vienna.

was a welcome exchange, however, as the publicity that his songs received through Vogl's performances was very useful.

"Schubertiads"

Schubert's circle of friends was still increasing – often through the introductions of Josef von Spaun. Friends and admirers met at various locations in Vienna. The meetings often took the form of concerts devoted to Schubert's music. These concerts became known as "Schubertiads."

Although Schubert composed for many years and produced many great works, he could never apply himself to seriously promoting his own work. This meant that he never made enough money to make a decent living from his music and constantly relied on friends for money and accommodation.

After the failure of Spaun's approach to Goethe, however, Schubert made attempts to interest publishers in *Erlkönig*. He wrote to the respected Leipzig firm of Breitkopf and Härtel. Unfortunately the manuscript was returned to another composer of the same name – Franz Schubert from Dresden. Herr Schubert from Dresden wrote indignantly to the publishers, "With amazement I must tell you that this cantata was never written by me. I shall retain it in my possession until I find out who has impertinently sent you this rubbish, and also the fellow who has thus misused my name." Eventually the manuscript was returned to Schubert without further comment.

Back to school

In August 1817, Schubert's room in the Schober household was needed by another member of the family and he had to leave. A little depressed, he returned again to his family home and once more took up the hated task of teaching.

The fact that he began, but never completed, two works during this period – a sonata and a new symphony – reflects this as a time of disappointment and frustration. But though Schubert was unhappy, musical society in Vienna at the time was joyous.

The operas of Rossini had taken Vienna by storm. Schubert himself was also impressed with Rossini's music and wrote two overtures "in the Italian style." One of these was Schubert's first work to be performed professionally. The important date was March 1, 1818.

Another encouragement this year was the appearance of Schubert's first published composition – the song *Erlafsee*. The publication in which the song appeared was a supplement to a magazine and was little-known, but nevertheless a composition was in print – at last!

Tutor

In July 1818, Schubert, now twenty-one, was offered the position of music teacher to the two daughters of Count Johann Karl Esterházy, Countess Marie and Countess Karoline, for the summer months. The Esterházys spent the summer in the country and returned, as was the fashion of the day, to their town residence for the winter. Schubert loved Vienna, and hated the thought of leaving the city, but finances urged him to accept the position.

On the positive side, accepting the post meant he would be able to resign from his father's school, yet still maintain a regular income. Also, he hoped that the peace and quiet of the country would enable him to do his work. For some years after Schubert had left the school, his father insisted on keeping his son's name on the staff list. Perhaps he saw a useful connection between the growing reputation of his son as a composer and the school.

The Esterházy chateau and estate was at Zseliz, in Hungary, three hundred miles (585km) from Vienna. Franz Schubert had never been so far away from home before and it was to be the furthest he would ever travel in his lifetime.

Life in the country

Even though he taught the countesses, Schubert was part of the Esterházy household staff and was only marginally higher in status than a servant. Most of

Schubert spent the summer of 1818 at the steward's lodge at Zseliz. Most of his compositions from this period are for piano duet, written for his two young piano students – the Countesses Marie and Karoline Esterházy.

the Esterházy employees lived in the steward's lodge in the castle grounds.

Here Schubert's room was fairly quiet except, it is said, for a flock of geese that occasionally made a terrible cackling noise and drowned out all conversation. Schubert found most of the other servants pleasant and made friends with the seventy-five year old surgeon. The two little countesses were "nice children." At first Schubert was very happy, and found life at Zseliz, with its beautiful grounds and gardens, fairly relaxed. By early August he was writing to friends, "I live and compose like a god," and asking for the message to be passed to his stepmother that his laundry was "very well looked after." He asked for new clothes to be sent to him, adding that he would forward the money at once – displaying a new financial confidence.

But, the situation soon changed. Schubert began to miss both his friends and Vienna very badly. There was no one on the estate to confide in, and the environment was becoming less easy for composition.

Vienna again

At the end of the summer the Esterházys returned to Vienna, where Schubert was retained in his position of teacher for the winter months. During this period he lodged with the poet Johann Mayrhofer. The two shared a room for the next two years, and got along reasonably well – helped by a particularly considerate landlady. Schubert had the use of a piano at Mayrhofer's lodgings, which made the working situation particularly good. Mayrhofer was a civil servant, and was out during the day, which gave Schubert the opportunity to write his compositions at the piano, undisturbed.

Comfortable lifestyle

Schubert's usual routine was to begin work in the morning and continue through to the afternoon. Then he would pay visits, meet friends, enjoy walks, and, later in the day, perhaps take in an opera or concert. To round off the evening, dinner was usually enjoyed at a local inn.

This was the way of life that Schubert loved. But the early mornings, when extra money could have been earned teaching, were wasted, as Schubert was not very good at getting up. Some of his friends

Schubert did take time off from composing to indulge some of his other interests. The Hinterbruehl Valley, south of Vienna, was visited and enjoyed by both Beethoven and Schubert. In one of the most beautiful cities of Europe, walking or riding were popular pastimes.

despaired of his lack of business sense. To Schubert, work was composition and he was simply not interested in anything else.

"I had no luck with the opera in Vienna.... I should be quite well if this wretched business of the opera were not so mortifying."

Franz Peter Schubert, in a letter to Spaun, December 7, 1822.

"The Magic Harp"

Once more settled in Vienna, and seeing the wealth of varied music-making around him, Schubert's thoughts turned again to opera. Opera was very important to the musical life of Vienna, and Schubert had always known that public recognition and acclaim would be his if he could write a successful opera. It was for this reason that he kept returning to this art form. He wrote seventeen operas in all – but only three of these were ever performed in his lifetime.

The limited success of *Die Zwillingsbrüder – The Twin Brothers* – which was completed in 1819, brought Schubert another commission. The request was to write incidental music for a three-act play, *Die Zauberharfe – The Magic Harp.*

In a fury of composition, Schubert completed the score in a mere two weeks. But after the first performance, the Viennese critics were again unenthusiastic. In reply to such adverse criticism, Schubert spoke to his friends of the "rot, enough to make your hair stand on end" that was being performed in Vienna instead of his own works.

The Opera House, Vienna, is one of the most famous opera houses in the world. Schubert always wanted to write a successful opera. The operas of Mozart were highly revered in Vienna at the time, and it is thought that his work The Magic Flute *particularly inspired Schubert's operatic ambitions.*

Politics

Nearing the end of his happy two years sharing an apartment with Johann Mayrhofer, Schubert was involved in his one skirmish with the police.

Mayrhofer was employed by the government as a censor of books to monitor what the public was allowed to read. But even as a civil servant, he felt that, along with his artist friends, he too was being watched. Suspicion within the intellectual world of artists and freethinkers was encouraged by the authorities – who believed that such people could be a threat to the government if they chose to challenge the system.

Chancellor Metternich distrusted all intellectuals, and it was almost inevitable that Schubert and his friends would at some time have a brush with the authorities. Fortunately this happened only once.

One morning in March 1820, Schubert was with a group of friends in rooms belonging to the poet Johann Senn, when the police burst in. Senn was accused of having spoken "rebellious thoughts" against the chief of police. In the pandemonium that broke out, Schubert received a black eye. Senn was arrested, along with Schubert and several of the others. Schubert was released later, but Senn was imprisoned for fourteen months for charges that were never proved. When he was finally freed, it was only to be exiled from Vienna for life. Schubert and he never met again.

Johann Mayrhofer, the poet and close friend of Schubert. The composer set forty-seven of Mayrhofer's poems to music, producing some of his most famous songs, such as Am See – By the Lake, *and* Abendstern – Evening Star.

In print

By 1821, the Schubertiad evenings were at the height of their popularity. Yet, although Schubert was slowly becoming a household name in Viennese musical society, so far not one of his songs had been published by a reputable music publisher.

As Schubert seemed to lack the confidence and business sense required to approach publishers himself, it was left once more to friends to take the lead. As *Erlkönig* was Schubert's most popular composition, it was decided to begin with that.

Accordingly, several publishers were approached, they included the well-established Tobias Haslinger

Because of his private personality, Schubert rarely tried to get his works performed in front of larger audiences, preferring instead the select audience of friends. During his own lifetime, he was little known outside the narrow limits of Viennese society.

and the equally respected Antonio Diabelli, neither of whom would accept the work. The song was repeatedly turned down – Schubert was "not well known enough," the song was entirely unsatisfactory for publication as the piano accompaniment was "too difficult."

In the end, Leopold von Sonnleithner and three other friends decided to publish the work themselves.

One hundred copies sold!

When, at a Schubertiad, it was announced that *Erlkönig* was available in print, most of those present eagerly rushed forward to buy copies, and almost one hundred of which were sold the same evening.

Everyone was delighted – and the money from the sales made it possible for the publication of further works. Twelve more songs were prepared for print. But this time, Diabelli – now more convinced of commercial success – agreed to distribute the music on a commission basis. The venture proved entirely successful. With the first payments they received, Schubert's friends immediately paid the debts with

which the composer constantly seemed to be associated. He could not be trusted to pay them himself. The remaining money was then given directly to Schubert.

This was a turning point in Schubert's career. Diabelli, finally assured that Schubert's music would sell, took on other publications at his own risk, and for the remainder of his life Schubert's works were published on a regular basis.

Schubert did, however, make one bad business agreement. At a time of poor personal finances, he sold the copyright of some of his earliest and best songs outright to Diabelli. This meant that he could no longer make any money from the pieces, and the agreement lost Schubert much-needed funds.

"The Atzenbrugg Feasts"

In the spring of 1821, Franz Schubert moved out of Johann Mayrhofer's apartment and into lodgings nearby. At twenty-four, the composer was living on his own for the first time.

During the year he spent much of his leisure time

Schubert was very shy and chary of talk. While sitting at the piano he would become very serious and as soon as his task was ended he would withdraw from the room. He seemed indifferent to praise and applause and indeed disliked people paying compliments."

Peter Gammond, from Schubert.

Schubert and his friends enjoyed an annual invitation by Schober's uncle to Atzenbrugg. The middle-class Viennese were well known for spending time enjoying themselves.

with Schober. In July, they went to Atzenbrugg, where they stayed in a small chateau on an estate managed by Schober's uncle. The castle was put at Schober's disposal each year and he invited friends to join him there. In their usual way of inventing names for people and events, Schober and his friends called these gatherings "The Atzenbrugg Feasts."

Later in the summer, Schober and Schubert teamed up to write an opera, which was to be "in the grand Italian style." Again they stayed at Atzenbrugg, later moving on to St. Pölten, where Schober's uncle was Bishop. Both venues brought them the peace and quiet they needed for writing.

"Alfonso und Estrella"

The opera was to be called *Alfonso und Estrella,* and the friends had high hopes for its production in Vienna. When they got back, Schubert moved into Schober's apartment so that they could work together. *Alfonso* was finished in February 1822, coinciding with a visit the composer Weber made to Vienna to conduct his opera *Der Freishütz.*

Both Schubert and Schober admired this opera, and Schober wrote a poem in praise of the composer, printed copies of which were scattered from the gallery after the performance of the opera. The

friends hoped Weber would offer help in obtaining a performance of their own opera. In the end, however, the hoped for help was unforthcoming, and *Alfonso und Estrella* was rejected for performance.

Schubert was deeply attached to the city of Vienna – its culture and its people – and spent his happiest moments in the company of friends there.

The "Unfinished Symphony"

After completing *Alfonso,* Schubert had a relatively quiet spring and summer. Later in the year, however, he began work in earnest on a new symphony. This symphony alone has since aroused more curiosity from musicians and biographers than any of his other works.

By the end of October the first two movements of the new Symphony in B minor were complete, and Schubert began work on the third movement, a light-hearted scherzo movement, but there his work on the symphony stopped. The next month Schubert concentrated on a new work, a magnificent piano piece – the *Wanderer* Fantasia. He never returned to the manuscript of his B minor symphony.

The following year, he gave the two completed movements to his friend Anselm Hüttenbrenner, with whom they remained for forty-three years, forgotten.

"Where others keep a diary in which they record their momentary feelings, Schubert confided his passing moods to music paper; his soul, musical through and through, wrote notes where others resort to words."

Robert Schumann, 1829.

So why did Schubert not complete the symphony? At some time during that year, he had contracted syphilis, a disease for which there was no cure at the time and which carried the likelihood of a painful death. Perhaps Schubert associated the depression that he felt during those months with the symphony he was composing, and was hesitant to return to it.

Poor health

Schubert was diagnosed as having syphilis during the winter of 1822–1823. It was after this that he decided to leave Schober's apartment and returned to live with his family, where he stayed for the next six months.

In a letter written to Schober at this time, he indicated in a single sentence that he was aware of the long-term character of the disease: "Whether I shall ever completely recover I am inclined to doubt. . . ." But despondent as Schubert clearly felt during this anxious period, he continued to produce works that were positive, and in no way artistically inferior to his earlier compositions.

An illustration of Schubert's song cycle, Die Schöne Müllerin. *In writing music for poetry, the composer found an important means of self expression. Schubert was also the first musician to treat the piano accompaniment and the words with equal importance.*

Determined

Still determined to crack the operatic nut, he composed two further stage works, *Fierabras – The Braggart* and *Die Verschworenen – The Conspirators.* But again, neither of these was accepted for performance. In the summer, however, he began a work that was to bring him considerable success – the song cycle, *Die Schöne Müllerin – The Beautiful Maid of the Mill.*

A song cycle is a series of songs based on poems that are linked by the same theme, or tell a story. The verses of *The Beautiful Maid of the Mill* are by the poet Wilhelm Müller, a contemporary of Schubert. Sadly, Müller, who like Schubert died young, never heard the song cycle performed.

On his return to Vienna after visiting Steyr and Linz with Michael Vogl, Schubert set about completing the songs. He was well enough to move out of the family home, and was again living on his

A mill such as this might have inspired the poet Müller to write Die Schöne Müllerin – The Beautiful Maid of the Mill, *on which Schubert based his song cycle of the same name.*

own. He had also accepted a commission to write incidental music for the dramatic work *Rosamunde*. This was at least performed – but only twice. It was to be his final completed dramatic work. In November, his health began to deteriorate again. The disease was progressing toward the end of its secondary stage, which brought with it the threat of illnesses such as hepatitis or meningitis.

No more Schubertiads

In the spring of 1824, Schubert, now twenty-seven, once again turned to writing instrumental music. By the end of March he had completed two string quartets – the A minor, and the famous *Death and the Maiden* quartet. This quartet uses music from the song of the same name, here rewritten as a theme and variations.

"In a word, I feel myself to be the most unhappy and wretched creature in the world. Imagine a man whose health will never be right again, and who, in sheer despair over this, ever makes things worse and worse, instead of better."

A letter from Schubert to Kupelwieser, March 31, 1824.

Franz Schubert with his friends Johann Baptist Jenger and composer Anselm Hüttenbrenner. Hüttenbrenner kept some of Schubert's works, such as the B minor Symphony, after the composer died.

As well as the depressive effect of his illness, Schubert was also saddened by the gradual breaking up of his circle of friends. The Schubertiad evenings grew fewer as various friends moved away from Vienna in the pursuit of their own lives and careers, and also to avoid the restrictions of the government. Spaun lived in Linz, Schober was working in Breslau, and Anselm Hüttenbrenner now held the position of music director in Graz, while Johann Senn, exiled from Vienna, lived in remote Tyrol.

But Schubert and his friends kept up a constant exchange of letters. Here Schubert shared his fears and hopes, "Each evening," he wrote to one friend, "when I retire to bed I hope I may not wake again."

"Between nine o'clock in the morning and two o'clock in the afternoon, Schubert daily and without exception devoted himself to composition or to his studies. But the afternoon and evening were given up to his family and friends.... To the beauties of nature he was most receptive, and on fine summer days he almost daily made longish excursions into the beautiful environs of Vienna."

A friend of Schubert, from a newspaper published soon after the composer's death.

Zseliz

By early summer, Schubert was once more music teacher for the Esterházys at Zseliz. This time as a "respected composer" he was given rooms in the castle itself. But it was not a happy time.

Again Schubert missed his close friends, and he was without anyone with whom he could have a "sensible word." His present life no longer seemed to interest him, and the future, because of his illness, even less. He constantly looked back to the happiness of past years.

Nevertheless the peace and tranquillity of Zseliz

The painted wall panels at Zseliz show the comfortable surroundings of the Austrian aristocracy and the rooms in which Schubert lived and worked. These scenes were far removed from his modest lodgings in Vienna.

seemed to do him good, and when he returned to Vienna in September his friends were pleased to see that he had regained some of his former bright self. His new compositions, too, seemed to be back in the old spirit. In November he composed a sonata for arpeggione, a curious instrument with six strings and frets, which is played like a cello.

By the end of the year, however, Schubert's health again failed. Blinding headaches returned and he was not well enough to attend a New Year party hosted by his colleagues. He grew detached and casual even to his closest friends.

Summer in Steyr

One of the friends who had warmly welcomed Schubert back to Vienna the previous year was the talented artist Moritz von Schwind, whom Schubert had met in 1821. Schwind was a young man of astounding talent – an artist foremost, but also a skilled composer. He and Schubert soon became

Salzburg, one of the cities visited by Schubert and Vogl during their summer tour. It was in Schubert's time that a month-long annual music festival was started. This still continues today, with concerts taking place throughout the city.

intimate friends – so much so that Schubert called him his "beloved."

In February 1825, the composer again moved out of his father's house, where he had stayed since his return from Zseliz, into new lodgings close to Schwind. The friends met daily, and the lack of substantial new compositions during the early part of the year suggests that there was plenty of socializing going on.

Concert tour

The summer brought a suggestion from Vogl that he and Schubert spend time together touring Austria – at Vogl's expense. It was decided that they would include a short concert tour – going to Linz, Gmunden, Salzburg, and Gastein – giving small concerts of Schubert's songs. Schubert was delighted by the way his songs were enjoyed by the provincial audiences. The song *Ave Maria* was particularly popular. In a letter to his parents, Schubert wrote that he came across his compositions "everywhere." For a time, at least, his health seemed to have stabilized.

Above: In 1825 Schubert set to music several songs from Sir Walter Scott's poem The Lady of the Lake, *including* Ave Maria. *When the songs were published it was intended that the original English text, as opposed to a German translation, should also be included to help popularize the songs in Britain.*

Above left: Schubert changed his lodgings frequently, and lived in many different houses and apartments. This shows the simple study where he lived in 1821.

Money problems

At the end of the tour, Schubert found to his delight that Schober had also returned to Vienna. Celebrations between the friends resulted in much merrymaking, continuing until the early hours. It is not surprising that Schubert, for the time being, found little time to compose.

By now, his reputation in Vienna was growing, and his music was published by four different publishers. But, again, money was in short supply. Schubert was still not earning enough from his music. His friends rallied around, trying to find a position for him, and when the post of Assistant *Kapellmeister* became vacant at the Court Chapel in 1826, Schubert agreed to apply. Irritatingly, the position was offered to someone else.

A second opportunity came when Schubert's friend Vogl recommended him as coach to one of the main Viennese orchestras. But Schubert's reaction at the audition did not do much to enhance his reputation. A singer complained that several notes in

Although it was not a large city, Vienna had four playhouses to support the demand for Italian opera and German drama. The Burgtheater, *shown above, was for spoken drama. Schubert and his friends would have attended such performances whenever they could afford to.*

the song he had written especially for the occasion were too high, and asked if they could be rewritten. Schubert refused, and walked out.

By July, the money situation was again serious. Schubert wrote to a friend, "I have no money at all, and things are going very badly for me. I do not worry about it and remain cheerful."

"Modern and difficult"

By 1826, although two more publishers were showing interest in his works, twenty-nine year old Franz Schubert was still not wholeheartedly accepted as a composer.

Publishers and concert-goers of the day also considered his music to be "modern and difficult." Some of his compositions were complicated to play. Schubert had already confessed this with regard to the piano accompaniment to *Erlkönig*. But Schubert, unlike some of his lesser contemporaries, made no attempt to please his audiences.

Although Schubert's last and greatest string

quartet – the String Quartet in G, written in a feverish two-week burst of activity in June – was reasonably well received at its private performance, he couldn't persuade anyone to publish it. It was too "harsh" and, quite simply, too original.

"My best hours here I owe to the unprinted works of Schubert of which I have quite a number at home in manuscript. Yet however delightful and enjoyable it is to contemplate them, everything about this music is sad."

Johannes Brahms, in a letter to his publisher, Reiter-Biedermann, 1862.

"Winterreise"

The next year Schubert was hard at work on a second song cycle, *Winterreise – The Winter's Journey.* The gloominess of the poetry seemed to affect him so much that Spaun asked him what was wrong. Schubert simply replied, "You will soon hear and understand." Some months later Schubert played through the new songs, and his friends were taken aback by the unusually gloomy overtones in the music. However, just as the composer had said, and with reinterpretations by Vogl, their original uncertain appreciation turned into full approval. Schubert considered the work to be his best yet.

Shortly after completing the first part of *Winterreise,* news came of Beethoven's rapidly deteriorating health, and on March 19, 1827 Schubert visited the dying composer. After so many hurried glimpses in the Viennese streets, Schubert at

The title page of Schubert's Variations in E minor, with a dedication to Beethoven. Despite Schubert's lifelong reverence for the Viennese master, this piece is the only dedication he made to him.

Above left: It was only when Beethoven was on his deathbed that Schubert was to finally meet the composer he most admired. The entire population of Vienna mourned when their greatest living composer died. Above top: Beethoven's funeral was attended by twenty thousand people.

last met Beethoven. Within a week, Beethoven was dead and the whole of Vienna was in mourning. Schubert was one of the torchbearers at Beethoven's grand and stately funeral.

House party

By March, Schubert was once again living with Schober. But now he had a sitting room, a bedroom, and a small music room for his own use. To someone used to small single rooms and shared garrets, this was accommodation on a large scale. He immediately gave a party for his friends – but when his guests arrived he was not at home to receive them! He had gone out, in an act of typical forgetfulness, only to meet up with everybody in the coffee house, by sheer coincidence, later in the evening.

During 1827, reports and reviews of Schubert concerts – on the whole reasonably positive – began to appear in several towns in Germany. Schubert's reputation was clearly spreading. There were also signs of his reputation in Vienna stabilizing, although many still thought of him only as a song composer.

The Viennese were famous for their love of conversation. To accommodate this need, there were over eighty coffeehouses, such as this one, in the city. In the last two years of his life, Schubert was to be seen at Bogner's practically every evening.

In June he was elected to the Vienna Music Society. Franz Schubert, just thirty years old, could not have realized or even suspected that he had barely more than a year to live.

"Franz Schubert's invitation concert"

After two successful public performances in January 1828, Schubert made plans for a major concert consisting solely of his own works. He chose the pieces with great care, deliberately adding some that he thought might be particularly popular. He decided to begin the concert with a movement from a new string quartet. The movement was long, which made him nervous about including the whole work. He followed this with songs, a trio, more songs, and finally a chorus for male voices.

All the plans went well, and the concert, which included Schubert himself as accompanist, played to a packed audience. Each piece was received with great enthusiasm, and the composer was called onto the platform to take the applause many times.

The evening was both a musical and financial success. Out of the takings Schubert received 320 florins. For once in his life he felt reasonably well

"I was in a state of bliss today. At the rehearsal a symphony by Franz Schubert was played.... It is gifted beyond measure."

Robert Schumann, in a letter to Clara Wieck, December 1839.

Above: "Crowding for a Schubert concert" – although Schubert never achieved the recognition he deserved during his lifetime, his music became increasingly popular as a result of his "Schubertiad" evenings and the publication of some of his works.

Opposite: The room in his brother's apartment where Schubert lived for the last few weeks of his life. When Schubert's talent began to be recognized after his death, many places associated with him were restored and preserved in his memory.

off. He used some of the money to pay off outstanding debts, and with the rest, after so many years playing on rented or borrowed instruments, he bought himself a piano.

But the concert was virtually ignored by the press. Vienna was now in a frenzy of musical excitement about the forthcoming visit of the violinist Niccolò Paganini. There was little space left in any of the newspapers for Austria's own Franz Schubert. It was the composer's first and last public concert.

Making money

The year 1828 saw great productivity for Franz Schubert. He completed his symphony, the "Great" C major. The composer Robert Schumann later commented that this work represented the very essence of Schubert. He also wrote the String Quintet, three piano sonatas, two major choral works, and thirteen songs. The songs were later published as *Schwanengesang – Swan Song.*

Schubert again tried to interest new publishers in

his works, and where successful, to obtain what advances against royalties he could. Composers were then – and still are today – paid royalties on the number of copies of their music that are sold. Sometimes publishers could be encouraged to pay an "advance" if they thought a work would sell well. Such a payment also served to encourage a successful composer to offer more works to that particular publisher. Schubert, like most composers, by far preferred an immediate payment rather than waiting months or even years for money.

For once Schubert's business efforts seemed to work, and he was approached by two respected German publishers. The letter from the company, Schott, was simply addressed to "Franz Schubert Esq., Famous Composer in Vienna." But, after lengthy dealings with both firms, Schubert only managed to interest the publishers in one piece. As today, publishers were often only prepared to print popular material that would sell easily – and Schubert didn't write much music like that.

Still working

There was no travel to alleviate work frustrations this year. The money was simply not available, nor was Schubert's health up to it.

In September his doctor suggested he moved out of the city into one of the suburbs. This he did, moving in with his brother Ferdinand and his family. But, although Ferdinand's house was close to the country and fresh air, the building was new and had not completely dried out. Furthermore, the sanitary facilities were unsatisfactory. This was not the place for a sick person.

Although his condition hadn't improved, Schubert continued to compose. At the end of September he played through three newly completed piano sonatas at a friend's house. Then, early in October, feeling slightly better, he went on a short walking tour with his brother and two colleagues, visiting Haydn's grave in Eisenstadt.

But the tour weakened his already ailing constitution. When he returned to Vienna, a letter awaited him inviting him to organize a concert of his songs in Pest, Hungary. In happier times this would have caused great excitement, but now Schubert was not well enough even to reply.

A nausea set in that was to be with him until his death. Dining at an inn one night, he took one mouthful of fish and was immediately revolted by it, saying the food tasted like poison. From then on Schubert ate virtually nothing. He took only medicine. Yet on November 3, he was still strong enough to attend a performance of a requiem mass written by Ferdinand, making the short journey on foot. The following day he made arrangements for several study sessions with a special music theorist.

Final days

On November 11, Schubert was too unwell to get up and had to be confined to his bed. The following day he wrote what was to be his last letter to Schober.

An engraving of Schubert, looking successful and confident, not showing the true situation of the composer – who had been passed by and neglected by his own Viennese public. In a city of high society, with its love of music on a grand scale, Schubert's quiet personality and his music for small audiences did not gain him much support or public acclaim while he was alive.

"Dear Schober, I am ill. Over the last eleven days I have had nothing to eat or drink. I can only walk from my chair to my bed and back.... Whenever I eat anything I am unable to keep it down. In my desperate plight, please be so kind and let me have some books...." He wanted books by James Fenimore Cooper, saying he had particularly liked *The Last of the Mohicans.*

During these last days Schubert was lovingly cared for by his brother Ferdinand and his young stepsister Josefa. He was frequently delirious, during which times he sang quietly to himself. When he was conscious, he spent time correcting the proofs of his last piece of music, *Winterreise.*

On November 16, Schubert's doctors held a consultation at his bedside, and diagnosed typhoid – a common cause of death in early nineteenth century Vienna. On the evening of November 17 Schubert's condition deteriorated rapidly, and from that time he never fully regained consciousness. Ferdinand

The house in which Schubert died. A real appreciation of Schubert's greatness did not come until more than forty years after his death, when the first biographies and extensive publications of his works placed his name among the other great composers.

recorded that during one of the composer's half-conscious moments, he indicated a wish to be buried next to Beethoven.

At three o'clock on Wednesday November 19, 1828, Franz Peter Schubert whispered, "Here is my end," and died. He was thirty-one years old.

Neglected affairs

After his death, Schubert's family and friends pieced together the composer's neglected affairs. The many unpaid bills reflected a lifestyle that had no interest in financial success. Money was owed to Franz Schober, to tailors and shoemakers, and to the piano repairer. In an effort to settle some debts, several manuscripts were sold to a publisher, but the works unfortunately raised very little funds.

The official summary and value of Schubert's estate indicated the extent of the composer's poverty; three cloth dresscoats, three frock-coats, ten pairs of trousers, five pairs of shoes, two pairs of boots, one hat, four shirts, nine neckerchiefs and handkerchiefs, thirteen pairs of socks, one sheet, two blanket cases, one mattress, one pillow, one blanket, and some old music books.

The clothes were shabby, the boots down-at-the-heel, the thin bed linen was barely warm enough to keep out the cold of a chilly summer night, the "old music books" consisted of a pile of used music paper. The official report valued Schubert's estate at a paltry sixty-three florins. The government inquirer questioned why there were no books of his works in the composer's effects. In fact Schubert's precious manuscripts had thankfully long since been safely removed by Ferdinand and placed with family and friends. The risk of them falling into the wrong hands otherwise was too great.

"Poor Schubert, so young and only at the beginning of a brilliant career. What a wealth of treasures his death has deprived us of."

Joseph von Spaun, on the death of Schubert.

"He died in his greatness"

According to his wish, Schubert was buried close to Beethoven. Only three graves separate the two great men. The organization required for this kind of burial added further to the funeral expenses. "Much! Very much! Yet surely very little for Franz," commented his father.

The Währing Cemetery, where Beethoven had been buried twenty months earlier, was situated on the other side of Vienna, several miles from where Schubert had died. The burial plot cost an extravagant thirty florins – almost half the composer's estate, and the removal of the body across the busy city added appreciably to the undertaker's charges. For his immediate friends and family Schubert's death had been costly.

Nevertheless it was fully understood, as well as being considered absolutely right, that Franz Schubert would have a respectable funeral with all the trappings of fashionable Vienna. There would be singing and a professional organist as well as wreaths, candles, and a "painted coffin with a

Opposite: Schubert's brief life was built around his love of composing. It is appropriate, then, that he should have been working on his compositions up to his death. His last song, Die Taubenpost – The Pigeon Post, *was written in October 1828, only a few weeks before he died.*

The monument to the composer in Schubert Park, where he was first buried. Later, his remains were transferred to the musician's section of Vienna's Central Cemetery to comply with his last wishes to be buried near Beethoven.

handsome pall." Franz Schober was requested to write words for the occasion, which were sung to Schubert's music.

So on November 21, 1828, a few weeks before what would have been Franz Schubert's thirty-second birthday, a group of students carried his coffin to the church of St. Joseph, in the Margareten area of Vienna. It was a stormy day, but the weather did not affect the dedication of the family, friends, and admirers that made up the long procession.

Schubert's death came as a terrible shock to his friends, many of whom had not realized his condition was so serious. In his diary Eduard von Bauernfeld wrote, "I wish I lay there in his place … for he leaves the world with fame." Moritz von Schwind commented simply, "Schubert is dead, and with him all that we had of the brightest and fairest."

"I have wept for him as if he was my brother, but I am glad that he has died in his greatness and has come to the end of his sorrows. The more I realize his nature, the more I see what he suffered. The memory of him will always be with us and all the troubles of the world will not prevent us from a deep feeling for all that has vanished with him."

Moritz von Schwind, in a letter to Schober.

Important dates

1797 Jan. 31: Franz Peter Schubert is born to Franz and Elizabeth Schubert in Vienna, Austria.

1802 At the age of five, Franz Schubert is introduced to the keyboard by his older brother, Ignaz.

1805 Franz Schubert, aged eight, sings in the choir of Liechtental church and is introduced to the violin by his father.

1808 Schubert successfully auditions for the choir of the Imperial Court Chapel and at the age of thirteen becomes a student of the Imperial and Royal City College in Vienna.

1810 Franz Schubert, aged eleven, writes some of his earliest surviving compositions, including a *Fantasie* for piano duet.

1811 Mar. 30: Schubert writes his earliest surviving complete songs, including *Hagars Klage – Hagar's Lament.*

1812 May 28: Franz Schubert's mother, Elizabeth, dies after a serious illness.
July 26: Schubert makes his last appearance as a chorister as his voice begins to break.

1813 Oct. 28: Schubert, aged sixteen, completes his First Symphony and dedicates this to the director of the *Konvikt,* Dr. Lang.
Schubert begins a teacher training course at St. Anna's College.

1814 Aug. 19: Schubert begins teaching at his father's school.
Oct. 16: Schubert's Mass in F, to commemorate the centenary celebrations of the Liechtental church, is performed to wide public acclaim.
Oct. 16: Schubert writes the song *Gretchen am Spinnrade – Gretchen at the Spinning Wheel,* based on the poem *Faust,* by Goethe.

1815 During the course of the year, Schubert completes two symphonies, two Masses, and about 145 new songs including *Erlkönig – The Erl King.*
Franz Schubert meets the poet Franz von Schober, who becomes a lifelong friend.

1816 Schubert completes symphonies four and five. He gives up teaching and moves to Schober's rooms to concentrate on composing.
June: Schubert composes his first paid commission, a cantata called *Prometheus.*

1817 Franz Schubert meets the singer Michael Vogl who becomes a close friend.

1818 Feb.: *Erlafsee* – the first of Schubert's songs to appear in print, is published.
Mar.: The first performance of one of Schubert's overtures, written in the Italian style of Rossini, is heard.
July: Schubert, aged twenty-one, is employed as a music tutor by the Esterházy family and moves to their chateau at Zseliz.

1819 Jan.: Schubert completes his first opera, a one-act farce, *Die Zwillingsbrüder – The Twin Brothers.*

1820 Aug.: Schubert's music for the play *Die Zauberharfe – The Magic Harp* is performed.

1821 At a "Schubertiad" evening, Schubert's friends announce that his song *Erlkönig* is available in print.
Franz Schubert meets Moritz von Schwind, an artist and composer who becomes a close friend.
Schubert and Schober begin work on the opera *Alfonso und Estrella.*

1822 Feb.: *Alfonso und Estrella* is rejected for performance. Schubert works on two movements of his Symphony in B minor, which he never completes.
Schubert writes the *Wanderer* Fantasy for piano.

1823 Schubert contracts syphilis.
Schubert begins work on the song cycle *Die Schöne Müllerin – The Beautiful Maid of the Mill,* and writes the music for the play *Rosamunde.*

1824 Schubert completes two string quartets in D minor and A minor.

1825 Schubert and his friend Vogl go on a concert tour, where Schubert's music is well received.

1826 Schubert writes the String Quartet in G but is unable to find a publisher for it.

1827 Schubert, aged thirty, composes *Winterreise – The Winter's Journey.*
Mar. 19: Schubert visits the dying Beethoven, whose work he has always admired.
June 12: Schubert is elected to the Vienna Music Society.

1828 Feb. 9: Schubert plays in his first and final public concert, in Vienna, to wide acclaim.
Schubert completes his C major Symphony, thirteen songs that later became known as *Schwanengesang – Swan Song.*
Nov. 19: Franz Peter Schubert, aged thirty-one, dies.

Recommended listening

Whither – This is the second song from the song-cycle *Die Schöne Müllerin – The Beautiful Maid of the Mill,* which tells the story of a miller's love for his master's daughter. He talks to the stream, which comforts him and becomes his friend. When the young girl falls in love with another admirer, he returns to the water and drowns himself, heartbroken. In this song the piano part depicts the flowing stream while the miller sings the tune.

Erlkönig – *The Erl King* – This is one of Schubert's greatest songs. The piano part has fast dramatic chords which set a mood of fear and agitation as the father gallops through the forest holding his small son. The singer has to play four roles: the narrator who tells the dreadful story, the boy who fears he is going to be stolen by a demon, the father who tries to comfort the child, and the Erl King himself. The piece is very difficult for both performers.

Marches Militaires – Marche Militaire in D – This is a piece for piano duet, which Schubert would have played with his own friends. The main tunes are played by the right-hand performer, while the player on the left accompanies with chords. It is a happy piece – a military march.

"Trout" Quintet – This was written for piano, violin, viola, cello, and double bass. In the last movement, Schubert uses a tune which he had composed two years earlier for a song called "The Trout." In the quintet Schubert uses this melody as a theme for variations. The theme is like a folk-song – simple and singable. As the variations progress, the tune is changed and elaborated.

Symphony in B minor ("Unfinished") Movement 1 – Schubert only finished the first two movements of this work. While he was working on the third movement, he found out that he had syphilis and would probably die from the disease. The first movement starts with a sad and haunting melody played by the cellos.

Glossary

Censorship: A means by which a publication can be withheld from the public by someone in authority.
Chamber music: Music written for a small group of musicians and instruments, each playing a separate part.
Civil servant: Someone who works in public service, administration or government.
Commission: To invite an artist or composer to write a piece or work, usually for a specified fee.
Copyright: The exclusive right given, by law, to a composer or writer to protect his or her work from being copied over a certain period of time.
Fantasia: An instrumental piece, usually for a solo instrument, in a style that is free and imaginative.
Fret: A ridge of ivory, metal or plastic on a string instrument, used to mark different pitches.
Harmony: When a combination of musical notes is played simultaneously, forming a chord. The term has come to signify the production of a pleasing sound combination.
Hepatitis: An illness caused by the inflammation of the liver.
Incidental music: Music to accompany a play.
Kapellmeister: The German name for the musical director of a chapel.
Key: The scale (a progression of notes in order of pitch) that the composer has chosen for a particular piece of music or melody.
Mass: The form of worship, usually in the Roman Catholic Church. The five main sections can be sung, usually in Latin, and may have an orchestral accompaniment.
Melody: A succession of musical notes that make up a piece of music.
Meningitis: An illness caused by an inflammation of the membranes that surround the brain.
Minor key: Music based on certain notes that form a minor scale.
Minuet: A piece of music in the style of the seventeenth and eighteenth century court dance.
Octet: A piece of music written for eight instruments.
Opera: A dramatic work in which all or most of the performers sing their parts.
Overture: A piece of orchestral music that introduces an *opera,* ballet, or other large work. An overture is often performed as a piece on its own.
Parnassus: A mountain in central Greece.
Patron: Someone who gives financial support to an artist or cause they feel is deserving.
Quartet: Music for four voices or four instruments.
Repertoire: A collection of works that an artist is able to perform.
Royalty: An agreed percentage of the cost of a piece of music that is paid to the composer every time a copy of the music is sold.
Score: The music, as written by the composer, showing each instrumental part. The instruments are always written in the same order down the page. The players themselves read from orchestral parts showing only their own music.
Sonata: A composition, made up of several parts, or movements, for a solo instrument or solo instrument and keyboard.
Song cycle: A set of songs that are usually associated by subject matter.
Soprano: The highest female singing voice.
Swan song: The last work of a person before their retirement or death.
Symphony: A long composition for orchestra, usually made up of four parts, or movements, for orchestra.
Theme: A group of notes that often provides the basis of a musical composition. A *melody*.
Transpose: To play or write a musical composition in a different *key* from the one in which the work was originally composed.
Triplets: A group of three notes played to the same value as two notes.
Variations: Modifications on a piece of music where the *theme* is repeated in a different, more elaborate, form.
Wind instuments: Any instrument that is sounded by using the breath, such as the woodwind or brass section of an orchestra.

Index